GoDaWork Conglomerate

Edition 64
Rise

Workbook for Genius Mindsets

Nicshelle A. Farrow M.A.Ed, Pi Lambda Theta

DEDICATION

To all of the thinkers with talent and creativity.

CONTENTS

Acknowledgments

1 Rise

2 Activities

3 Create Your Impact

*About the Author

ACKNOWLEDGMENTS

To all that naturally give their all for
the greater good!

1 RISE

What does this word mean to you?

How do you feel about this word?

Why is this word impactful?

Where will you use this word?

Exemplify how you can benefit
from this word.

Why will you begin to accentuate this word?

2 ACTIVITIES

Draw your envisioned picture of this word.

Research the origin of this word.

Create your own game using your research.

____

____

____

____

____

____

____

____

____

Design a Logo

Write a Motivational Speech

Build a form of technology.

Create a Script!

Write a Short Story!

3 CREATE YOUR IMPACT UPON THE WORLD

-DRAW, WRITE A POEM, SONG, OR MORE

ABOUT THE AUTHOR

Nicshelle A. Farrow M.A.Ed, Pi Lambda Theta

Nicshelle is a community advocate. She is one of the most highly energetic motivators you will meet! Nicshelle's smile, energy, encompassing her plethora of educational experiences will indeed leave participants eager to level up individually or in any organization. She also tutors and leads acting classes that support elevating literacy in communities at large. In addition, Nicshelle has a monumental amount of virtual documentation of her love for creativity and work toward improving global literacy as she advertises enthusiastically through entertainment, education, and entrepreneurship.

www.ingramcontent.com/pod-product-compliance
Lightning Source LLC
Chambersburg PA
CBHW070224180726
47999CB00017B/2303